WINTER SPORTS

by Finley Fraser

Consultant: Beth Gambro
Reading Specialist, Yorkville, Illinois

BEARPORT
PUBLISHING

Minneapolis, Minnesota

Teaching Tips

Before Reading

- Look at the cover of the book. Discuss the picture and the title.

- Ask readers to brainstorm a list of what they already know about winter sports. What can they expect to see in the book?

- Go on a picture walk, looking through the pictures to discuss vocabulary and make predictions about the text.

During Reading

- Read for purpose. Encourage readers to think about winter sports as they are reading.

- Ask readers to look for the details of the book. What is happening?

- If readers encounter an unknown word, ask them to look at the sounds in the word. Then, ask them to look at the rest of the page. Are there any clues to help them understand?

After Reading

- Encourage readers to pick a buddy and reread the book together.

- Ask readers to name three sports from the book that they can do during winter. Go back and find the pages that tell about these sports.

- Ask readers to write or draw something they learned about winter sports.

Credits:
Cover and Title page, © iStock/Artranq; 3, © Shutterstock/monticello; 5, © iStock/manonallard; 7, © Shutterstock/strgaphoto; 9, © iStock/FatCamera; 10, © Shutterstock/Lucky Business; 11, © Shutterstock/Sergey Novikov, © Shutterstock/Sashkin; 12, © iStock/Joseph Calomeni; 13, © Shutterstock/Dan Thornberg; 14, © Shutterstock/Sergey Novikov; 17, © Shutterstock/Vadim Zakharishchev; 18–19, © iStock/AlexD75, © Shutterstock/Ari N; 21, © Shutterstock/BlueSkyImage; 22, Public Domain, © Shutterstock/monticello; 23, © Shutterstock/Kirill Spiridonov, © Shutterstock/Billion Photos, © Shutterstock/Vaclav Volrab, © Shutterstock/Pressmaster

Library of Congress Cataloging-in-Publication Data

Names: Fraser, Finley, 1972- author.
Title: Winter sports / by Finley Fraser.
Description: Bearcub Books Edition. | Minneapolis, Minnesota :
  Bearport Publishing Company, [2021] | Series: Seasons of Fun: Winter |
  Includes bibliographical references and index.
Identifiers: LCCN 2021009281 (print) | LCCN 2021009282 (ebook) | ISBN
  9781647478872 (Library Binding) | ISBN 9781647478926 (Paperback) | ISBN
  9781647478971 (eBook)
Subjects: LCSH: Winter sports--Juvenile literature. | Skating--Juvenile
  literature. | Hockey--Juvenile literature. | Skis and skiing--Juvenile
  literature. | Snowboarding--Juvenile literature. | Snowshoes and
  snowshoeing--Juvenile literature. | Sledding--Juvenile literature. |
  Illustrated children's books.
Classification: LCC GV841.15 .F73 2021 (print) | LCC GV841.15 (ebook) |
  DDC 796.9--dc23
LC record available at https://lccn.loc.gov/2021009281
LC ebook record available at https://lccn.loc .gov/2021009282

For more information, write to Bearport Publishing, 5357 Penn Avenue South, Minneapolis, MN 55419.

Contents

Playing Sports

It is time for winter fun!

There are many sports to play in the winter.

Which sport will I play?

Ice skating is fun!

I put on my skates.

They have sharp **blades**.

I tie them up tight.

First, I take small steps on the ice.

Then, I **glide** from one foot to the other.

Whoosh!

I am skating!

My friend plays hockey.

She wears a **helmet** and **pads** to stay safe.

She uses her hockey stick to hit the **puck**.

Basketball is fun, too!

My school has a team in the winter.

I pass the ball to my friend.

He shoots the ball.

He scores!

When it snows, my brother likes to ski.

He wears a helmet to stay safe.

He zooms over the snow.

My brother is so fast!

My sister likes to snowboard.

She wears a helmet like my brother does.

She goes fast, too.

Sometimes my brother and sister race!

Do you want to snowshoe?

We wear special shoes.

They help us walk on top of the snow!

Winter sports are so much fun!

I want to try them all.

Which winter sport do you like best?

The Story of Ice Skates

Ice skating started more than 3,000 years ago!

The first ice skates were made from the bones of animals. People put the bones on their shoes to glide on ice!

Today's ice skates have sharp blades made from metal.

Glossary

blades thin, flat parts on the bottom of skates

glide to move smoothly

helmet a hard hat worn to keep the head safe

pads things worn to keep the body safe

puck the hard rubber disk that is used in hockey

Index

Read More

Manley, Erika S. *Figure Skating (I Love Sports).* Minneapolis: Jump!, Inc., 2018.

Sherman, Jill. *Hockey (Blastoff! Readers: Let's Play Sports).* Minneapolis: Bellwether Media, 2020.

Learn More Online

1. Go to www.factsurfer.com
2. Enter "**Winter Sports**" into the search box.
3. Click on the cover of this book to see a list of websites.

About the Author

Finley Fraser is a writer and snowshoeing enthusiast living in Portland, Maine. He once tried skiing, but it didn't go very well!